LIFE PICTURE PUZZLE

WELCOME TO LIFE'S TWELFTH PICTURE PUZZLE BOOK

Who would have thunk it? When we released our first LIFE Picture Puzzle book all those years ago, we suspected we were on to a good thing, and when it went to number one on *The New York Times* best-seller list, we were suitably thrilled. But we had no idea that, 12 books later, the franchise would still be going strong. To paraphrase the words of a famous Oscar winner, "You like us, you really like us." And we like you: We feel it's a privilege to continue to craft these puzzles, and it feels like we're getting back together with old friends as we issue this twelfth book in the series.

When our team started to plan the new book, all sorts of ideas for a new theme were tossed around. The word *extraordinary* kept coming up: "Isn't it extraordinary—12 books." "It's extraordinary how much people like these puzzles—kids and adults alike." Going with what was in the air, we asked our photo editors to start looking for extraordinary—and extraordinarily fun—images from around the world. They came up with many surprising, wonderful pictures, and we sat down to work. On the pages that follow is the result, and it's fair to say that we are just as proud of this book as we were of our first.

The theme may be new, but the hallmarks of the LIFE Picture Puzzle series haven't changed. Our Novice section is still a kind of tutorial, wherein we present the easiest puzzles for our beginning players. Our Master and Expert sections slowly dial up the difficulty, preparing you for the increasingly difficult challenges to come. Then there's our Genius section. We feel we should give you fair warning about this chapter: The Genius puzzles are so difficult that even our Puzzle Master sometimes has trouble finding all the changes when he returns for a second or third look. And he's the one who hid them in the first place!

[OUR CUT-UP PUZZLES: EASY AS 1-2-3]

We snipped a photo into four or six pieces. Then we rearranged the pieces and numbered them.

Your mission: Beneath each cut-up puzzle, write the number of the piece in the box where it belongs.

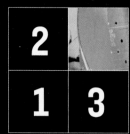

Check the answer key at the back of the book to see what the reassembled image looks like.

[HOW TO PLAY THE PUZZLES]

Jumping for Joy . . .

. . . and bragging rights back at the stables

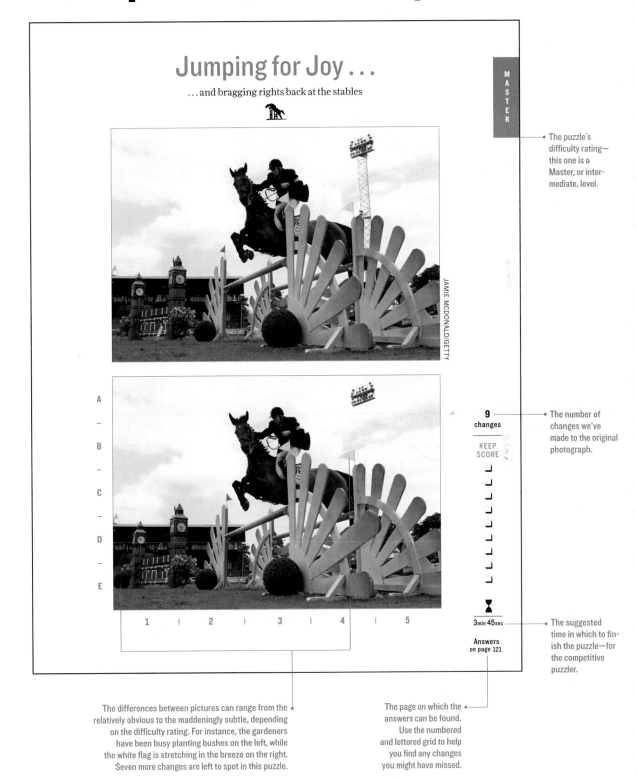

JAMIE MCDONALD/GETTY

MASTER — The puzzle's difficulty rating— this one is a Master, or inter- mediate, level.

9 changes — The number of changes we've made to the original photograph.

KEEP SCORE

3min 45sec — The suggested time in which to fin- ish the puzzle—for the competitive puzzler.

Answers on page 121

The differences between pictures can range from the relatively obvious to the maddeningly subtle, depending on the difficulty rating. For instance, the gardeners have been busy planting bushes on the left, while the white flag is stretching in the breeze on the right. Seven more changes are left to spot in this puzzle.

The page on which the answers can be found. Use the numbered and lettered grid to help you find any changes you might have missed.

LIFE PICTURE PUZZLE

Puzzle Master Michael Roseman
Editor Robert Sullivan
Director of Photography Barbara Baker Burrows
Deputy Picture Editor Christina Lieberman
Copy Editors Marilyn Fu, Barbara Gogan, Parlan McGaw

LIFE Puzzle Books
Managing Editor Bill Shapiro

LIFE Books
President Andrew Blau
Business Manager Roger Adler
Business Development Manager Jeff Burak

Editorial Operations
Richard K. Prue (Director), Brian Fellows (Manager), Keith Aurelio, Charlotte Coco, Tracey Eure, Kevin Hart, Mert Kerimoglu, Rosalie Khan, Patricia Koh, Marco Lau, Brian Mai, Po Fung Ng, Rudi Papiri, Robert Pizaro, Barry Pribula, Clara Renauro, Hia Tan, Vaune Trachtman

Time Home Entertainment
Publisher Richard Fraiman
General Manager Steven Sandonato
Executive Director, Marketing Services Carol Pittard
Director, Retail & Special Sales Tom Mifsud
Director, New Product Development Peter Harper
Director, Bookazine Development & Marketing Laura Adam
Publishing Director Joy Butts
Assistant General Counsel Helen Wan
Book Production Manager Suzanne Janso
Design & Prepress Manager Anne-Michelle Gallero
Brand Manager Roshni Patel

Special thanks to Christine Austin, Jeremy Biloon, Glenn Buonocore, Jim Childs, Susan Chodakiewicz, Rose Cirrincione, Jacqueline Fitzgerald, Christine Font, Carrie Frazier, Lauren Hall, Malena Jones, Mona Li, Robert Marasco, Kimberly Marshall, Amy Migliaccio, Nina Mistry, Brooke Reger, Dave Rozzelle, Ilene Schreider, Adriana Tierno, Alex Voznesenskiy, Vanessa Wu

PUBLISHED BY

LIFE Books

an imprint of Time Home Entertainment Inc.   Vol. 11, No. 3 • June 10, 2011

Copyright © 2010
Time Home Entertainment Inc.
135 West 50th Street
New York, NY 10020

We welcome your comments and suggestions about LIFE Books. Please write to us at:
LIFE Books
Attention: Book Editors
PO Box 11016
Des Moines, IA 50336-1016

If you would like to order any of our hardcover Collector's Edition books, please call us at 1-800-327-6388 (Monday through Friday, 7 a.m. to 8 p.m., or Saturday, 7 a.m. to 6 p.m. Central Time).

COVER: ANDREY SMIRNOV/AFP/GETTY

READY, SET,

GO!

NOVICE

[These puzzles are for everyone: rookies and veterans, young and old. Start here, and sharpen your skills.]

Baa, Baa, Yellow Sheep

This puzzle's dyed in the wool

JON FURNISS/WIREIMAGE/GETTY

7
changes

KEEP
SCORE

⏳

1min 50sec

Answers
on page 121

Head Shot

Sometimes getting a good photo requires
a change of perspective

A
–
B
–
C
–
D
–
E

1　　2　　3　　4　　5

9
changes

⏳

2min 35sec

Answers
on page 121

KEEP SCORE ★ ❏ ❏ ❏ ❏ ❏ ❏ ❏ ❏ ❏

I, Robot

You, puny puzzle-solving humans

A

B

C

D

E

1   2   3   4   5

6
changes

KEEP
SCORE

❏
❏
❏
❏
❏
❏

⏳
1min **45**sec

Answers
on page 121

One-Trick Pony

If they cross the finish line together,
does it still count?

MOHAMMED MAHJOUB/AFP/GETTY

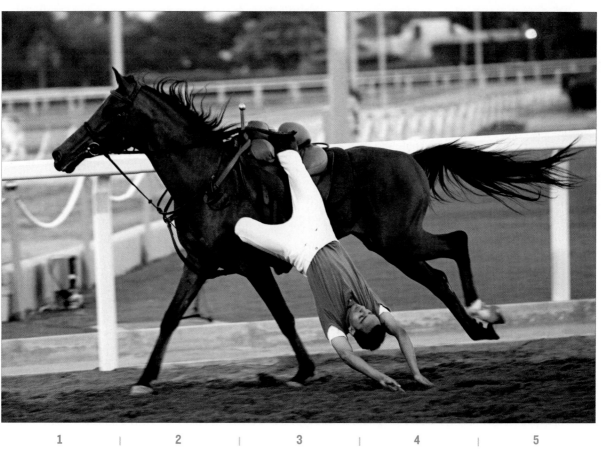

A
–
B
–
C
–
D
–
E

1　　2　　3　　4　　5

7
changes

⧖

2min 25sec

Answers
on page 121

KEEP SCORE ★ ❏ ❏ ❏ ❏ ❏ ❏ ❏

Sky Jockey

She's spinning more than just her wheels

AFP/GETTY

A
–
B
–
C
–
D
–
E

1   2   3   4   5

9
changes

⧗

2min 40sec

Answers
on page 121

KEEP SCORE ★ ❑ ❑ ❑ ❑ ❑ ❑ ❑ ❑ ❑

As He Takes Flight

You flag the photo that doesn't fit

1

2

3

4

5

6

⧗
0min **25**sec

Answer
on page 121

PIERRE-PHILIPPE MARCOU/AFP/GETTY

Group Bliss

These couples are perfect matches, and so are five of the pictures

1

2

3

4

5

6

STR/AFP/GETTY

0min 40sec

Answer
on page 121

Puttin' On the Ritz

This family is all dressed up *and* has somewhere to go

A

B

C

D

E

1   2   3   4   5

8
changes

KEEP
SCORE

❑
❑
❑
❑
❑
❑
❑
❑

⌛

2min 20sec

Answers
on page 121

Horsing Around

Who's the beast of burden here?

A
—
B
—
C
—
D
—
E

1 | 2 | 3 | 4 | 5

6
changes

⧗
2min 15sec

Answers
on page 121

KEEP SCORE ★ ❏ ❏ ❏ ❏ ❏ ❏

Must-See TV

He's not your standard couch potato

A
B
C
D
E

1   2   3   4   5

8
changes

⧖

2min 45sec

Answers
on page 121

KEEP SCORE ★ ❏ ❏ ❏ ❏ ❏ ❏ ❏ ❏

Sunday in the Park ...

... with Rex

NORBERT MILLAUER/AFP/GETTY

8
changes

KEEP
SCORE

❏
❏
❏
❏
❏
❏
❏
❏

2min 35sec

Answers
on page 122

A
—
B
—
C
—
D
—
E

1 | 2 | 3 | 4 | 5

In Search of Perfect Powder

Boldly going where no skier has gone before

A
—
B
—
C
—
D
—
E

1   2   3   4   5

6
changes

KEEP
SCORE

❑
❑
❑
❑
❑
❑

⧗

3min 25sec

Answers
on page 122

Catch of the Day

There's a lot that's fishy about this photo

9
changes

KEEP
SCORE

❏
❏
❏
❏
❏
❏
❏
❏
❏

⧗

2min 35sec

Answers
on page 122

Guardian Angel

Everyone feels safer with their flying pig
patrolling up above

A

B

C

D

E

1   2   3   4   5

11
changes

⏳

4min 10sec

Answers
on page 122

KEEP SCORE ★ ❏ ❏ ❏ ❏ ❏ ❏ ❏ ❏ ❏ ❏ ❏

Hitchhikers in the Sky

Either that or the flight was overbooked

DIGITAL VISION/GETTY

A

—

B

—

C

—

D

—

E

1   2   3   4   5

10
changes

⧗
3min 50sec

Answers
on page 122

KEEP SCORE ★ ❏ ❏ ❏ ❏ ❏ ❏ ❏ ❏ ❏ ❏

House of Slytherin?

Let's hope they can parse Parseltongue

9
changes

KEEP
SCORE

❑
❑
❑
❑
❑
❑
❑
❑
❑

⌛

3min 15sec

Answers
on page 122

Hold On Tight!

From this point on, it's all downhill

TORU YAMANAKA/AFP/GETTY

8
changes

⧗

3min 30sec

Answers
on page 122

KEEP SCORE ★ ❑ ❑ ❑ ❑ ❑ ❑ ❑ ❑

Party Girls, GOP-Style

Yes, it's true. They like Ike.

10
changes

KEEP
SCORE

❑
❑
❑
❑
❑
❑
❑
❑
❑
❑

⌛

2min 55sec

Answers
on page 122

Hoping for the Big Bounce

Can you reconnect the biker to his bungee cord before sudden impact?

LUTZ BONGARTS/BONGARTS/GETTY

⏳

0min 25sec

Answer
on page 122

KEEP SCORE

Superhero in Training

Here's a second high-flyer who needs help

OLIVIER RENCK/AURORA/GETTY

KEEP SCORE

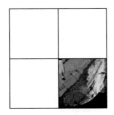

0min 45sec

Answer
on page 122

All Eyes on Big Ben

The times they are a-changin' in olde London towne

CARL DE SOUZA/AFP/GETTY

A

B

C

D

E

1 | 2 | 3 | 4 | 5

12
changes

KEEP
SCORE

❏
❏
❏
❏
❏
❏
❏
❏
❏
❏
❏
❏

⏳
4min 25sec

Answers
on page 122

MASTER

[
Here, puzzles get
a little harder. You'll
need to raise
your game a level.
]

In the Pink

It's smooth sailing for this funny bunny

ISIFA/LIBOR FOJTIK/GETTY

A

—

B

—

C

—

D

—

E

1 | 2 | 3 | 4 | 5

11
changes

KEEP
SCORE

❑
❑
❑
❑
❑
❑
❑
❑
❑
❑
❑

⏳

4 min 25 sec

Answers
on page 123

Risky Business

He goes bang for a living, five times a day

A

B

C

D

E

1 | 2 | 3 | 4 | 5

9
changes

KEEP
SCORE

❏
❏
❏
❏
❏
❏
❏
❏
❏

⧗

3min 45sec

Answers
on page 123

Talk About a Hybrid

This is the perfect house for someone always on the go

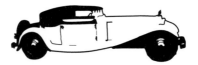

A
—
B
—
C
—
D
—
E

1 | 2 | 3 | 4 | 5

11
changes

3min 15sec

Answers
on page 123

KEEP SCORE ★ ❑ ❑ ❑ ❑ ❑ ❑ ❑ ❑ ❑ ❑ ❑

When Pigs Fly . . .
. . . so will I

A
—
B
—
C
—
D
—
E

1 | 2 | 3 | 4 | 5

9
changes

⧗
3min 25sec

Answers
on page 123

KEEP SCORE ★ ❑ ❑ ❑ ❑ ❑ ❑ ❑ ❑ ❑

On the Monkey Bars

Where's the missing link between the two gymnasts?

9
changes

KEEP
SCORE

⏳
2min 55sec

Answers
on page 123

A | B | C | D | E

5 | 4 | 3 | 2 | 1

Ding-Dong! The Witch Is Dead

She's not only merely dead,
she's really most sincerely dead

A
—
B
—
C
—
D
—
E

1   2   3   4   5

10 changes

⧗

3min 40sec

Answers
on page 123

KEEP SCORE ★ ❏ ❏ ❏ ❏ ❏ ❏ ❏ ❏ ❏ ❏

Not-So-Skinny Dipping

In Japan, things are going swimmingly for these two

SANKEI/GETTY

A
–
B
–
C
–
D
–
E

1 | 2 | 3 | 4 | 5

12
changes

KEEP
SCORE

3min 55sec

Answers
on page 123

Horns of Plenty

Reminds us of a certain cough drop commercial

THOMAS LOHNES/AFP/GETTY

10
changes

KEEP
SCORE

☐ ☐ ☐ ☐ ☐ ☐ ☐ ☐ ☐ ☐

3min 35sec

Answers
on page 123

A | B | C | D | E

1 | 2 | 3 | 4 | 5

Caution! Baby (Giraffe) Onboard

This little lady's definitely a head-turner

A

B

C

D

E

1   2   3   4   5

9
changes

⧗

2min 50sec

Answers
on page 123

KEEP SCORE ★ ❑ ❑ ❑ ❑ ❑ ❑ ❑ ❑ ❑

Making Like Jonah

This exhibit tells a whale of a tale

A
–
B
–
C
–
D
–
E

1 | 2 | 3 | 4 | 5

10
changes

⧗
3min 25sec

Answers
on page 124

KEEP SCORE ★ ❏ ❏ ❏ ❏ ❏ ❏ ❏ ❏ ❏ ❏

Traffic Jam

Can you spot which picture sails away from the others?

1

2

3

4

5

6

0min 35sec

Answer
on page 124

CARLOS ALVAREZ/GETTY

Doggie Diplomacy

Five pooches vote "Aye," one votes "Nay"

1

2

3

4

5

6

LUCAS DAWSON/GETTY

0min 50sec

Answer
on page 124

And the Band Played On

Here's hoping they finish before the tide comes in

A
—
B
—
C
—
D
—
E

1 | 2 | 3 | 4 | 5

10
changes

KEEP
SCORE

❏
❏
❏
❏
❏
❏
❏
❏
❏
❏

⧗

3min 25sec

Answers
on page 124

Tipping Point

Time to sue the architect!

SEAN GALLUP/GETTY

A

B

C

D

E

1   2   3   4   5

9
changes

⧗

3min 55sec

Answers
on page 124

KEEP SCORE ★ ❏ ❏ ❏ ❏ ❏ ❏ ❏ ❏ ❏

Spin Cycle

Around and around he goes

GREG WOOD/AFP/GETTY

10
changes

KEEP
SCORE

4min 15sec

Answers
on page 124

Canal Concerto

Find the altered image and you can toot your own horn

1

2

3

4

5

6

1min 15sec

Answer
on page 124

MARCO SABADIN/AFP/GETTY

The Weather Outside Is Frightful

But come on in, the water's fine

1

2

3

4

5

6

1min 10sec

Answer
on page 124

Flipping Flapjacks

As in most things, practice makes perfect

A —

B —

C —

D —

E

1 | 2 | 3 | 4 | 5

9
changes

⧗

3min 35sec

Answers
on page 124

KEEP SCORE ★ ❑ ❑ ❑ ❑ ❑ ❑ ❑ ❑ ❑

Moving Day

You're the contractor, now build the house

JENS-ULRICH KOCH/AFP/GETTY

KEEP SCORE

Don't Look Down Now

Acrophobics may want to skip this puzzle

SCOTT OLSON/GETTY

KEEP SCORE

1min 10sec

Answer
on page 124

Birds Do It, Bees Do It

Even statues in the trees do it

12
changes

KEEP
SCORE

3min 50sec

Answers
on page 124

EXPERT

[Only serious puzzlers
dare to tread past this point.
Who's in?]

Some Really Great Pumpkins

Where is Linus when you need him?

JOE BOMBA/BOMBA PHOTOS

KEEP SCORE

3min 45sec

Answer
on page 125

Stupid Human Tricks

Just feed him candy and he'll roll over every time

BEN HIDER/GETTY

A
—
B
—
C
—
D
—
E

1 | 2 | 3 | 4 | 5

13
changes

KEEP
SCORE

❏
❏
❏
❏
❏
❏
❏
❏
❏
❏
❏
❏
❏

⧗
4min 10sec

Answers
on page 125

A Hair-Raising Competition

Talk about a stiff upper lip

WILDBILD/AFP/GETTY

12
changes

KEEP
SCORE

❏
❏
❏
❏
❏
❏
❏
❏
❏
❏
❏
❏

⏳

3min 50sec

Answers
on page 125

Rack 'Em Up

Can you run the table on this puzzle?

A
—
B
—
C
—
D
—
E

1 | 2 | 3 | 4 | 5

15
changes

KEEP
SCORE

❏
❏
❏
❏
❏
❏
❏
❏
❏
❏
❏
❏
❏
❏
❏

⧗

4min 35sec

Answers
on page 125

Gourds A-Plenty

Five sets are the same. Which isn't?

1

2

3

4

5

6

1min 45sec

Answer
on page 125

LIBOR FOJTIK/ISIFA/GETTY

Be-Side Saddle

He's either performing a stunt or looking for a high five

1

2

3

4

5

6

FERENC ISZA/AFP/GETTY

2min 5sec

Answer
on page 125

Spick-and-Span

As they say, cleanliness is next to clownliness

13
changes

KEEP
SCORE

4min 45sec

Answers
on page 125

REM

These kids are keeping their eye on you

SCOTT OLSON/GETTY

A — B — C — D — E

1   2   3   4   5

14 changes

⧗

4min **50**sec

Answers on page 125

KEEP SCORE ★ ❏ ❏ ❏ ❏ ❏ ❏ ❏ ❏ ❏ ❏ ❏ ❏ ❏ ❏

Moon Over Down Under

Remember, the opera in Sydney, too, ain't over until the fat lady sings

TORSTEN BLACKWOOD/AFP/GETTY

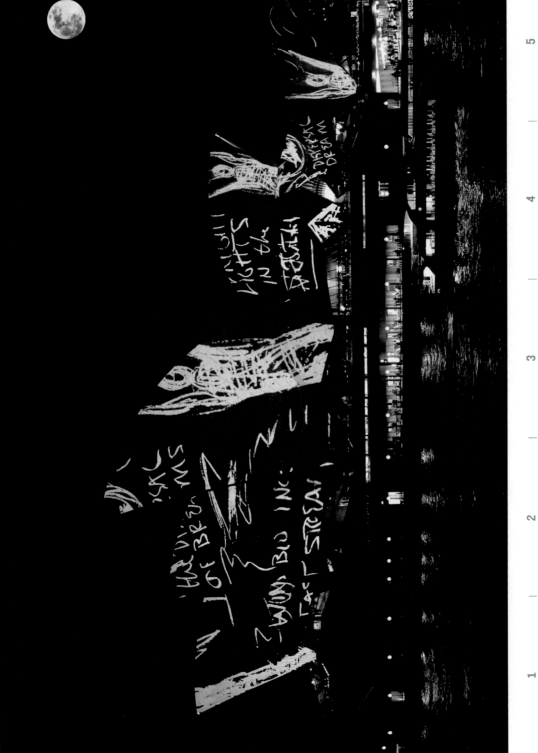

A   B   C   D   E

1   2   3   4   5

EXPERT

14
changes

KEEP
SCORE

❏ ❏ ❏ ❏ ❏ ❏ ❏ ❏ ❏ ❏ ❏ ❏ ❏ ❏

⧗
5min 15sec

Answers
on page 125

GENIUS

[
Finding a single difference
in these puzzles is a
challenge. Finding them all
might be impossible.
]

Pedestrian Crosswalk

He knows enough to wait for the light

LISA MAREE WILLIAMS/GETTY

A

B

C

D

E

1   2   3   4   5

13
changes

KEEP
SCORE

⏳
4min 25sec

Answers
on page 126

Dizzy Yet?

It's like riding inside a very large washing machine. A top-loader.

LEON NEAL/AFP/GETTY

5

4

3

2

1

A

B

C

D

E

14
changes

KEEP
SCORE

❏ ❏ ❏ ❏ ❏ ❏ ❏ ❏ ❏ ❏ ❏ ❏ ❏ ❏

⌛

5min 5sec

Answers
on page 126

Fixer-Uppers

They may look a bit shabby,
but just think of the resale potential

A

—

B

—

C

—

D

—

E

1   2   3   4   5

15
changes

⧗

5min 15sec

Answers
on page 126

KEEP SCORE ★ ❑ ❑ ❑ ❑ ❑ ❑ ❑ ❑ ❑ ❑ ❑ ❑ ❑ ❑ ❑

Iron Chef

You need a stomach of steel for his chow

A

B

C

D

E

1 2 3 4 5

16
changes

5min 25sec

Answers
on page 126

KEEP SCORE ★ ❏ ❏ ❏ ❏ ❏ ❏ ❏ ❏ ❏ ❏ ❏ ❏ ❏ ❏ ❏ ❏ ❏ ❏

A Favorable Wind

One photo isn't getting quite as much lift

1

2

3

4

5

6

2min 30sec

Answer
on page 126

PHILIPPE HUGUEN/AFP/GETTY

On a Wing and a Prayer

Plane truth: Only five of these are the same

1

2

3

4

5

6

SHAUN CURRY/AFP/GETTY

2min 45sec

Answer
on page 126

In-Flight Dining

Did you know that food is less caloric at altitude?

SEAN GALLUP/GETTY

A   B   C   D   E

1   2   3   4   5

16
changes

KEEP
SCORE

☐ ☐ ☐ ☐ ☐ ☐ ☐ ☐ ☐ ☐ ☐ ☐ ☐ ☐ ☐ ☐

⌛
5min 55sec

Answers
on page 126

Cheek to Jowl

It's one way of making new friends

A

B

C

D

E

1   2   3   4   5

16
changes

KEEP
SCORE

⬛
⬛
⬛
⬛
⬛
⬛
⬛
⬛
⬛
⬛
⬛
⬛
⬛
⬛
⬛
⬛

⌛

5min 15sec

Answers
on page 126

Right of Way

This would be the wrong time
for a mechanical mouse to show up

JIM DYSON/GETTY

20 changes

KEEP SCORE

☐ ☐ ☐ ☐ ☐ ☐ ☐ ☐ ☐ ☐ ☐ ☐ ☐ ☐ ☐ ☐ ☐ ☐ ☐ ☐

⏳ 6min 35sec

Answers on page 127

A | B | C | D | E

1 | 2 | 3 | 4 | 5

LIFE
CLASSICS

[These puzzles were
specially created with
memorable photos
from the LIFE archives.]

Will Work for Peanuts

Because there is no elephant minimum wage

WALLACE G. LEVISON/DAHLSTROM COLLECTION

A

B

C

D

E

1   2   3   4   5

10
changes

KEEP
SCORE

❏
❏
❏
❏
❏
❏
❏
❏
❏
❏

⧗

2min 45sec

Answers
on page 127

Strategic Air Command

These future aviators of America have big dreams

CHARLES STEINHEIMER/LIFE

A

—

B

—

C

—

D

—

E

1 | 2 | 3 | 4 | 5

11
changes

⧗

4min 10sec

Answers
on page 127

KEEP SCORE ★ ❑ ❑ ❑ ❑ ❑ ❑ ❑ ❑ ❑ ❑ ❑

Aqua-Cat

He bravely goes where no feline has gone before

GREY VILLET/LIFE

A

–

B

–

C

–

D

–

E

1 | 2 | 3 | 4 | 5

9
changes

KEEP
SCORE

❏
❏
❏
❏
❏
❏
❏
❏
❏

⧗

2min 15sec

Answers
on page 127

Heaven's Angels

The boys are eating their dust

A
—
B
—
C
—
D
—
E

1 | 2 | 3 | 4 | 5

12
changes

⧗
4min 35sec

Answers
on page 127

KEEP SCORE ★ ❏ ❏ ❏ ❏ ❏ ❏ ❏ ❏ ❏ ❏ ❏ ❏

Under the Big Top

It's the greatest show on the third rock from the Sun

RALPH MORSE/LIFE

A
—
B
—
C
—
D
—
E

1 | 2 | 3 | 4 | 5

9
changes

⧗
3min 50sec

Answers
on page 127

KEEP SCORE ★ ☐ ☐ ☐ ☐ ☐ ☐ ☐ ☐ ☐

[ANSWERS]

Finished already? Let's see how you did.

[INTRODUCTION]

Page 3: **Jumping for Joy . . .**
No. 1 (A2): This horsey's ear is getting just a bit larger. No. 2 (A4 to C4): These lights don't need no stinking tower. No. 3 (B3): Four-legs may not know it, but two-legs's reign ended with the snapping of the reins. No. 4 (B4): Flapping in the breeze has stretched out this flag. No. 5 (C2): The wind seems to have changed direction. No. 6 (C3): A hoof has hoofed its way out of the image. No. 7 (D4): The spoke has delusions of wooden grandeur. Nos. 8 and 9 (E1): The gardeners have planted another shrub, while the number sign has had its last countdown.

[NOVICE]

Page 7: **Baa, Baa, Yellow Sheep** No. 1 (A4): Can you see the fridge now? No. 2 (B1 to B2): It's a sure sign of reversal. No. 3 (B3): They need to repost the poster. No. 4 (B5): That's what we call back to the future. No. 5 (C1): She's either turning the other cheek or shaking her head at the whole sorry parade. No. 6 (E2): This one seems to have an invisible hoof. No. 7 (E4 to E5): It's just like dyeing an Easter egg, but how do you dip the sheep?

Page 8: **Head Shot** No. 1 (A1 to A2): The kiosk is in the purple these days. No. 2 (A3): Don't count on getting more than one photo from this booth. No. 3 (A3 to B3): The reflection is now just a flection. No. 4 (A4): Gee, what's holding up the roof? No. 5 (B1 to B2): This shot looks familiar somehow. No. 6 (C2 to D2): It's good to take a stand, just not this stand. No. 7 (C3): She's bucked off her buckle. No. 8 (D1 to D2): His shirt sleeve is peeking out. No. 9 (E4): The cable snakes inside the stand.

Page 10: **I, Robot** No. 1 (B2 to D4): This 'bot must have growing pains. No. 2 (B3): All these changing acronyms are very confusing. No. 3 (C3): Is it a good sign that the wing on his abdomen now points up? No. 4 (E1): They're cutting back the lighting to save on the electric bill. No. 5 (E3): That's also why the lights are going off in the city. No. 6 (E5): But just in case the darkness causes any unrest, they've beefed up security.

Page 12: **One-Trick Pony** No. 1 (A5): The lights start going on automatically at dusk. Nos. 2 and 3 (B1): The nose knows that there's one ring less. No. 4 (B3): How does he bend his foot down like that? No. 5 (C3 to D4): Changing the color of your shirt while hanging upside down from a horse—now that's a trick. Nos. 6 and 7 (D5): As the horse lost a hoof, the post must have slipped backward.

Page 14: **Sky Jockey** No. 1 (A1): The release handle has been skyjacked. No. 2 (B1): You've heard of hair extensions? Well, this is a wing extension. Nos. 3 and 4 (B5): Careless, careless. This plane has lost both a logo and a wing. Nos. 5 and 6 (C2 to D2): We've taken away a reflection but given the planes a longer runway. No. 7 (C3): A crooked smile is part of her charm. No. 8 (C4): When the blood rushes to your brain, colors may seem to change. No. 9 (D3): Flipping numbers are another sign of upside-downitis.

Page 16: **As He Takes Flight**
A cross in photo No. 6 is rotating.

Page 17: **Group Bliss**
The bride in photo No. 4 is going to be quite upset when she realizes she's lost her tiara.

Page 18: **Puttin' On the Ritz** No. 1 (B1): The light is being restored. No. 2 (B4 to C4): A tourist has popped up out of nowhere. No. 3 (B5): How will they know that it's a tea room? No. 4 (C2): She's bobbled the bauble. No. 5 (C4): The mask is winking. No. 6 (C5): Someone is freshening up. No. 7 (E2): The fake sapphire has been replaced by a fake ruby. No. 8 (E5): There's a new diamond on the floor.

Page 20: **Horsing Around** No. 1 (A3): Now this horse is spotless. No. 2 (A4): A tree grows . . . somewhere. No. 3 (C3): We've got to rein in the disappearing stud. No. 4 (D2): Stealth leather casts no shadow. No. 5 (D4): He's tooting on a longer flute. No. 6 (E2 to E3): Ancient Hungarian proverb: Grass grows swiftly over a resting hoof.

Page 22: **Must-See TV** No. 1 (A3): There's no such thing as too many guns on the wall. No. 2 (B1): A painting must have fallen down. Nos. 3 and 4 (B4): The painting has slipped down, and the bison's horn is growing. No. 5 (C5): He likes watching himself on the nanny cam. No. 6 (D1): The recliner has lost its footrest. No. 7 (D2): It's a cloven hoof no more. No. 8 (D3 to D4): When the bison gets bored he starts flipping his chain.

Page 24: Sunday in the Park . . . No. 1 (A4): Now, that's a bad case of red-eye. No. 2 (B5): Does anyone know a good veterinary dentist? No. 3 (C3): His arm may be small but those claws are large. Where is he hiding it? No. 4 (D2 to E2): The park has these new floating signs. No. 5 (D4 to E4): Her back must be aching. No. 6 (D5): His backpack sports a mood stripe. Nos. 7 and 8 (E4): With all the hopping around, the boy seems to have lost his patch.

Page 25: In Search of Perfect Powder No. 1 (A2 to B1): The copter has two new spotlights. No. 2 (A2 to B2): The antenna has squirted its last message. So goes its shadow. No. 3 (B1): Gain more light, lose a blade. Oops! No. 4 (C5): This blade is trying hard to compensate for the missing one on the other side. No. 5 (D1 to E1): The mountains are on the rise. No. 6 (D4 to E4): The pole is a bit shorter now.

Page 26: Catch of the Day No. 1 (A2 to A3): That's a whale of a tail. Well, actually, it's a shark of a tail. No. 2 (B1): The chimney has one less stack. No. 3 (B5 to C4): Less rain will get in now. No. 4 (C3): The plumbers put in another vent line. No. 5 (D1): It's a big pane in the glass. No. 6 (D1 to E1): The door has a brand-new paint job. No. 7 (E1): Apparently, a wheel has been withdrawn. No. 8 (E2): Car logos come and go. No. 9 (E3): Knock on wood that gate is solid.

Page 28: Guardian Angel No. 1 (A3): Something seems to have alarmed the flying pig. No. 2 (B2): The swiped light wasn't bright, so its sudden absence won't bring on night. No. 3 (B3): The rare and diminutive third nostril is sometimes known as a nostrilette. No. 4 (C3): This little piggie's leg hopped all the way home. No. 5 (C4): Suddenly he's got a hoofier hoof. No. 6 (D1): A red interloper has slipped into this gathering of Golden Delicious apples. No. 7 (D2): A wooden pole has rising ambitions. No. 8 (D3): She likes to stick with basic black. No. 9 (D4): He likes this sweater so much he owns one in every color. No. 10 (D5): It's a high-hat garbage can. No. 11 (E3): This is what happens when you let funhouse employees paint your signs.

Page 30: Hitchhikers in the Sky No. 1 (A3): He must be double-jointed. No. 2 (B4 to B5): Jumpers take care! On the way down, don't get caught on the overly long tail whatchamacallit, oh, the horizontal stabilizer. No. 3 (C1): He never learned the importance of opposable thumbs. No. 4 (C2): If the dial's danger zone is no longer red, does that mean it's safe now? Nos. 5, 6, and 7 (C3): With the whatever-it's-called missing, falling may be an option (research informs us that it's the starboard stabilizer. *Great*). But don't worry, the purple goggles will help. *Right*. Still, the binocular camera will capture all the action on the way down. No. 8 (C4): By the time we count to 10, that cloud better be back in place. No. 9 (D1): A rivet has bolted. No. 10 (D5): The forest road has been overgrown.

Page 32: House of Slytherin? Nos. 1 and 2 (A3): Watch out! Snakes always roll their eyes before they strike. And sometimes they stick out extra tongues. No. 3 (B2): The spire sticks up. No. 4 (B4): A leopard may not change its spots, but this snake can. Nos. 5 and 6 (D2): The shadow gets bigger as the sleeve gets longer. No. 7 (D2 to E2): She carries several purses with her just for occasions like this. No. 8 (E4): This slate tile has more weight. No. 9 (E5): And this little tile is missing.

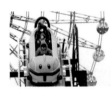

Page 34: Hold On Tight! No. 1 (A1): The missing strut was a spare. We hope. No. 2 (A2): That's a big hoodie. No. 3 (A5 to B5): This cab is hanging on the outside of the Ferris wheel. No. 4 (B2): She's so excited, she's looking both ways. No. 5 (C1): Better get an electrician up here before sunset. No. 6 (D2): The coaster car looks a bit worried. No. 7 (D3): He thinks he's a big wheel. Oh, he is. No. 8 (E2): The bumper has extra padding now.

Page 36: Party Girls, GOP-Style No. 1 (A1 to B1): Mr. Chairman, Kentucky casts all 56 votes for the next President of the United States . . . No. 2 (A3 to B3): That *S* is a bit slippery. Nos. 3 and 4 (A3 to A4): The green triangle points up. No. 5 (A4): A light has blown. No. 6 (B3 to C3): She's letting her hair down. No. 7 (B4): Stick with who? Or is it whom? *Copy!* No. 8 (C4): Yeah, lost earrings are very dependable puzzle changes. No. 9 (D2 to D3): If her skirt keeps getting shorter, she may be in trouble by the end of the night. No. 10 (E4): Don't look now, but this girl is really a flamingo.

Page 38: Hoping for the Big Bounce

4	1
3	2

Page 39: Superhero in Training

4	2
1	3

Page 40: All Eyes on Big Ben Nos. 1 and 2 (A4): Big Ben is less pointed these days, and bigger windows are in vogue. No. 3 (A5 to B5): The louvers are doing a handstand. Without any hands. No. 4 (B3): Let's all get together and do the checkerboard flip. No. 5 (C2): It looks like they bought the third hand secondhand. No. 6 (C4 to C5): Windows are another favorite object for puzzle changes. No. 7 (C4 to D4): The metal frame is a bit greenish.

No. 8 (C5 to D5): By now you must have realized that the character *S* is a very slippery critter in puzzle-land. No. 9 (D2): The latticework on the columns is getting a bit too ornate. No. 10 (D4 to E5): It's a good thing that the missing wheel is just a fake. Nos. 11 and 12 (D5): With a little bit of effort, an *E* becomes an *L* and a ladder loses its step.

[MASTER]

Page 43: **In the Pink** No. 1 (A1 to B4): There's one steeple more, we must confess. No. 2 (A5): With one steeple less, that evens the score. No. 3 (B1): The tree has been efficiently depruned. No. 4 (B5): In violation of fire regulations, a chimney has been removed and is currently being held in detention, awaiting trial by a jury of its peers. No. 5 (C3): This large-eyed bunny sees all—and he's not very happy about it. No. 6 (C5): Three windows must be better than two. Nos. 7 and 8 (D1): More boats can now tie up on the farther shore, and Mr. Swivel-Hips seems surprised about it. No. 9 (D3): What's he pointing at? No. 10 (D4): Oh, he's pointing out the hovering STOP sign. No. 11 (E3): Old Pink Skin is nursing a swollen paw.

Page 44: **Risky Business** No. 1 (A1 to B2): And upward through the air he flew. No. 2 (A1): He's so relaxed, he has time to wave hello to family and friends. Or is it goodbye? No. 3 (B2): Many human cannon balls have twitchy feet. Well, wouldn't you? No. 4 (B5): The force of the cannon blast has blown the top right off this tree. No. 5 (D4 to E5): It's quite a solid stripe. Nos. 6 and 7 (E1): It looks like a mysterious individual both planted a new tree and sliced away the spotlight's pole. No. 8 (E4): One of the cannon's decals has been looking in the mirror too much. No. 9 (E4 to E5): In compensation, another decal has been slapped on.

Page 46: **Talk About a Hybrid** No. 1 (A3): The VW house's stack has slipped a bit. It must be buggy. No. 2 (A4): The new chimney is the standard two-vent model. No. 3 (B1): Skylights are easy come, easy go around here. No. 4 (B2): They're also slippery when wet. No. 5 (B2 to B3): The windshield/window has been shuttered for the evening. No. 6 (B4): The side view sports a few more louvers now. No. 7 (B5): See what we mean about skylights. No. 8 (C1 to C2): Please return the window before we have to search you for it. No. 9 (C4): The staircase is going stealth on us. No. 10 (D4): The hubcap blinders are closing. No. 11 (E2 to E3): Mind the extra step.

Page 48: **When Pigs Fly . . .** No. 1 (A1 to B1): He's rapidly distancing himself from this mess. No. 2 (A2): When the helmet turns green, it's time to scream. No. 3 (A4 to B4): Someone's brother has joined the team. No. 4 (B3): It looks like he's trying to flap his wings. Good luck with that. No. 5 (B4): Now who's going to time the crash? Nos. 6 and 7 (D3): This is neither the time nor place to start losing wheels or growing teeth. No. 8 (D4): Even plastic pigs can suffer from lazy eye, especially under stress. No. 9 (E1): Relax, it's just one of our standard window additions.

Page 50: **On the Monkey Bars** No. 1 (A1 to A2): You never know when you're going to want a bit of extra rope, do you? No. 2 (B2 to B3): If he can smile holding himself upside down in the air, he must be having fun. No. 3 (B3): That solves a knotty problem and reduces the chance of getting splinters. No. 4 (D1 to E1): The pole bars the bar. No. 5 (D2): One blocked hole has stopped the drainage flow. No. 6 (D5): The rope is out of the loop. No. 7 (E3): Either the end of this bar is invisible or someone's about to take a spill. Nos. 8 and 9 (E5): The orangutan is holding the ends together as a platform floats away.

Page 52: **Ding-Dong! The Witch Is Dead** No. 1 (A2): Another darn letter has contracted the irreversible reversing disease. No. 2 (A3): Thankfully, ruby slippers come in large, extra-large, and ridiculously large sizes. No. 3 (B5): Vampires stalk the streets of New York City. Watch for their reflections— or lack thereof. Makes it kind of difficult, doesn't it? Nos. 4 and 5 (C2): As a truck teeters on the edge, a man goes strapless. Or at least his bag does. No. 6 (C3): Keep your eyes on the hand. What hand? Exactly. No. 7 (C4): They'll even steal the faces off of the posters around here. No. 8 (D1): If you throw off a sandal, just keep walking. No. 9 (D2 to E2): The crack got whacked. No. 10 (D3): The witch is a little less of a heel.

Page 54: **Not-So-Skinny Dipping** No. 1 (B1): This umbrella seems pointless. No. 2 (C1): Lost: Tip of tail. Reward offered. No. 3 (C3): Shake a leg so the trunk can hide. No. 4 (D1): Congratulations! You've put your thumb on the change. No. 5 (D2): The pole has an automated spinning crook. No. 6 (D4): Bigger bags hold more shells. No. 7 (D5): The rope done broke. No. 8 (D5 to E5): The poncho is seaweed green. Nos. 9 and 10 (E1): Both the umbrella tip and the pants cuff are extra-long. No. 11 (E3): Salt water has shrunk his pants. No. 12 (E4 to E5): Her smock has sagged.

Page 56: **Horns of Plenty** No. 1 (A1): It's another of those pesky skylight changes. Our bad. No. 2 (A4): The others make fun of his featherless headgear. No. 3 (B2): Where did it go, the missing pole? No. 4 (B4): This fellow keeps double-time. No. 5 (B5): Does anyone have a needle and some thread? Perhaps an extra button? No. 6 (C3): This section of the curb has been solidified. No. 7 (D1): With his larger instrument, he really gets to horn in. No. 8 (D1 to E1): This horn has been illuminated. No. 9 (D3 to E4): The shadow rules. No. 10 (E2): Someone gets a star for effort.

Page 58: **Caution! Baby (Giraffe) Onboard** No. 1 (A3 to B3): She's either shaking her head no or making sure she doesn't miss anything. No. 2 (C1): The exhaust pipe twists in the breeze. No. 3 (C3 to D3): If you can read this sign, you're in trouble. No. 4 (C3): Also, did anyone run a spellchecker on it. No. 5 (D4): Ntombi is a bit south of here. Nos. 6, 7, and 8 (E1): Okay, the cab's rear light is gone, a flasher's been added to the scene, and the red flag is really red. No. 9 (E5): A car has just pulled up and parked.

Page 60: Making Like Jonah No. 1 (A3): *Quick!* From the look of the spine, this fellow needs emergency chiropractic intervention. No. 2 (A5): The column is shrinking with age. It happens to a lot of us. Nos. 3 and 4 (B5): As the upper jaw jutted forward, the lower jaw lost a loose tooth. No. 5 (C2): A man has vanished in the light. No. 6 (D1): Its short fin can no longer swim. No. 7 (D4): A bone is wrapping itself around the step ladder. No. 8 (E3): His hair is turning brown. It must be winter. Nos. 9 and 10 (E4): Without four legs, the ladder is turning yellow.

Page 62: Traffic Jam
In photo No. 2 a boat has hit rock-bottom, leaving its sail behind.

Page 63: Doggie Diplomacy
A brand-new panoramic picture window adorns the building in photo No. 6.

Page 64: And the Band Played On No. 1 (C3): When she picked her bow, she got the short end of the stick. No. 2 (C4): Forget music! He could make millions from his hair-restoration formula. No. 3 (D1): The beachcomber is making his way along the surf. No. 4 (D2): The pegbox and scroll are away on vacation. No. 5 (D3): Now she's dressed in style. No. 6 (D4): His jacket is slowly wrapping itself around him. Hint: Never buy a tux made from python skin, even if it's on sale. Nos. 7 and 8 (D5): The box has popped two pegs and this stroller looks oddly familiar. No. 9 (E3): The foam is on the roam. No. 10 (E4): The tux's tail is more available now.

Page 66: Tipping Point No. 1 (A1 to B2): After consultations with the builders, the roof has taken a new angle on things. No. 2 (A2): One of the air conditioners is on the move. No. 3 (A3): Snip, snip with the scissors, and say goodbye to the cord. Just make sure the power is off first. Or call the electrician. No. 4 (B2 to B3): There's a new shadow on that old window of mine. No. 5 (B4): Their carpenter is named Johnny On-the-Spot. No. 6 (D3): Take a peek inside. It must be furniture moving day. Be thankful you're outside. No. 7 (E1): The eucalyptus bush is growing apace. No. 8 (E3): Instead of trying to use a short fence pole, just return it to the manufacturer. No. 9 (E5): It's getting sandier outside the fence.

Page 68: Spin Cycle No. 1 (A3 to B4): It looks like he's going for the almost-impossible dreaded double-flip. Nos. 2 and 3 (B3): The spin cycle has flung off a fender while someone raised a flag. No. 4 (C1 to D1): Taller towers have more power to gaze down upon the land. No. 5 (C5 to D5): We wonder what's hidden inside the sealed arch.

No. 6 (D4 to D5): Just apply a few bricks and, voilà, a window no more. No. 7 (D5): There's someone peeking out of the open window. No. 8 (E1): If there's a media event without a cameraman, does it really happen? No. 9 (E3): The landing gear has more reach. No. 10 (E4): The copter has an unlisted call number.

Page 70: Canal Concerto
Photo No. 3 is shy one vessel.

Page 71: The Weather Outside Is Frightful
The man in photo No. 5 doesn't have a leg to stand on.

Page 72: Flipping Flapjacks No. 1 (A1 to B1): These kids are under the watchful eyes of the church. No. 2 (B3 to C3): Flip them fast enough and you'll double your reward. No. 3 (C3): The flapjack is on the rise. No. 4 (C5): It's the case of the incredible shrinking pan. No. 5 (D3): He's elbowing his way in. No. 6 (D5 to E5): This pan has vanished all together. No. 7 (E2): Hey, who ate my pancake? Nos. 8 and 9 (E3): One girl is so happy, she could just float. Oh, she is. The other lass is stepping forward.

Page 74: Moving Day

3	6
2	5
1	4

Page 75: Don't Look Down Now

5	3
1	6
2	4

Page 76: Birds Do It, Bees Do It No. 1 (A2 to B2): An arborist has been busy with shears. No. 2 (B2): She's donated her thumb to a good cause. No. 3 (B5): Somewhere someone is feasting on a giant box of chocolates. No. 4 (C1 to D2): Hemlines are lower this year. No. 5 (C3 to D3): She's a giant to her people. No. 6 (C4 to D4): This lady is a quick-change artist. Can you make a living at that? No. 7 (C5 to D5): Fewer buildings create a more pastoral feeling. No. 8 (D2): The sign has signed off. No. 9 (D3): It's a long, long, long sleeve. No. 10 (E2): Her strap has snapped. No. 11 (E4): He's slowly

subsiding into the wood. No. 12 (E5): The tree prop is in retreat.

[EXPERT]

Page 79: Some Really Great Pumpkins

5	8	2
1	7	4
3	6	9

Page 80: Stupid Human Tricks No. 1 (A2): A street light has been removed to reduce urban light pollution. Can you see the stars? No. 2 (A3): The lazy dog's tongue lolls loosely over her lips. *Lots of laughs.* No. 3 (A5): Is it a sign that the sign is gone? No. 4 (B1 to C2): She's traded in her bag for a slimline version. No. 5 (C1): The metal bar has been bent around the wooden rail. No. 6 (C3): Don't trip on the orange stripe. No. 7 (C3 to D3): Someone's foot has beat a hasty retreat. Nos. 8 and 9 (C4): The pooch is a little leggy and a shoestring needs replacement. No. 10 (C5 to D5): Termites seem to be busily undermining this post. No. 11 (D1): The metal barrier has taken a wider stance. No. 12 (D4): Good, good, good. Play with Frisbee now, now. Frisbee now, please. No. 13 (E4): The sleeve is a smidge longer. Just a smidge.

Page 82: A Hair-Raising Competition Nos. 1 and 2 (A2): The hat is a little less distinguished now, and so is Mr. Unibrow. No. 3 (A4): Now, this is a real top hat! Well, it's not a bottom hat, is it? No. 4 (B4): He should see things more clearly now. No. 5 (B5): He's given his hair a whirl to give it more curl. No. 6 (E1): Button's been banished. No. 7 (E2 to E4): Two numbers have swapped. No. 8 (E2): Infinity beckons. Nos. 9, 10, 11, and 12 (E4): A white dot is not, the cord's been snipped, the 7 has been mirror-fied, and the logo, if not the product, has gone green.

Page 84: Rack 'Em Up No. 1 (A1 to A3): Isn't this lamp shade a bit bigger than necessary? No. 2 (A3 to A4): The latticework spreads like a virus. No. 3 (A5): We snapped the chain, but we did not snap the pole below. No. 4 (B1): He may be caged, but at least he's clear of the table. Nos. 5, 6, and 7 (B2): The microphone has lost its logo, a ball has bounced into view, and someone's entered the room. Nos. 8 and 9 (B4): The blue ball rolls, and a witness vanishes. No. 10 (B5): The red ball has left the table. No. 11 (C1 to C2): The chair is impaired. No. 12 (C5): He must be holding his leg out. No. 13 (D2): Another small silvery object is kaput. No. 14 (D5): Now he knows how much time he's wasting. No. 15 (E4): He's been there so long his shoe size has gone up.

Page 86: Gourds A-Plenty
Photo No. 3 is no longer in the fried chicken business.

Page 87: Be-Side Saddle
The sock in photo No. 2 is held up with Velcro.

Page 88: Spick-and-Span No. 1 (B1): The malleable shoe art has shifted its point of view. No. 2 (B1 to B2): I'm sorry, sir, but track information is currently unavailable and will remain so for the indefinite future. Have a nice day! No. 3 (B2 to C2): He's slipped on a blue wristband. No. 4 (B3): A clown is still a clown no matter the color of his nose. No. 5 (B5): Just hang your coat . . . where? No. 6 (C2): The sock is going over to the dark side. No. 7 (C2 to D2): A shy shoe has hidden its toe. No. 8 (C3): A festive event like this calls for earrings. No. 9 (C3 to D4): She looks good in leggings of any color. No. 10 (C4): Her bangle is true-blue. No. 11 (E1): After a while there was just one tile. No. 12 (E3): It's hard to believe her shoe size could get any bigger. No. 13 (E4): Some of this strap could really be trimmed away.

Page 90: REM Nos. 1 and 2 (A2): A reliable chimney removal and a window merge start out this eye-popping puzzle. Nos. 3 and 4 (A3 to C4): The roving eye is now wearing a green contact. No. 5 (A5): This window would rather reflect clouds. No. 6 (B1): The roof is singing the Jackie Wilson song "Higher and Higher." No. 7 (C1): Shut that window right now! Good. No. 8 (D2 to E2): His larger size will help stem the big eye roll. No. 9 (D3): Help, help! She's dropped her book. No. 10 (E1): The car has hit the road, Jack. Nos. 11 and 12 (E3): Her pants grow long as he cautiously turns around. No. 13 (E4): Where is she hiding her bag? No. 14 (E5): Here's a freebie: His shirt is purple. Well, what did you expect? It was free.

Page 92: Moon Over Down Under No. 1 (A5): It's moonrise over the harbor. No. 2 (B1 to C1): One of the famous roof shells is suffering from inflation. No. 3 (B2 to C2): With just a sleight of hand, a *D* becomes a *B*. Gee. No. 4 (C2): The *W* has been blown away. Get it? Can you explain it to us? Nos. 5 and 6 (C4): Another light-man has joined the gang, so turn on more than one light. Nos. 7 and 8 (D2): One more lamp has been installed on the promenade and one window removed. No. 9 (D3): Lose a window, gain, well, another window. Okay, you try making these changes sometime. Nos. 10 and 11 (D5): We're down to a single dream now. Choose wisely. But at least there's an extra doorway to handle the crowds. No. 12 (E3): A reflection of light on the water has been misplaced. If you find it, let us know. No. 13 (E4): Remember the old childhood game of Red Light, Green Light? Here it's done up in lights. No. 14 (E5): The boat has a Roman nose now. Or is it a Roman bow?

[GENIUS]

Page 95: Pedestrian Crosswalk No. 1 (A3): It must have taken a really tall truck to sheer off part of this traffic light. No. 2 (B1): Don't you think these new bricks match the old ones perfectly? Nos. 3, 4, and 5 (B3): As the roof drops, the jaws snap shut, and an eye begins to glow. No. 6 (C5 to D5): Telescopic tails were unusual anatomical additions in the late Jurassic. No. 7 (D1): Hope that car didn't go too far. It's our escape vehicle. No. 8 (D2): This bumper has less opportunity to vent now. No. 9 (D3): The hubcap has been sacked. No. 10 (D4): Even an ancient dino needs its thumbs. No. 11 (D5 to E5): Big, beautiful dino seeks chunky shadow for LTR. No. 12 (E2): This *O* has filled in quite a bit. No. 13 (E4 to E5): We just love adding extra digits on critters.

Page 96: Dizzy Yet? No. 1 (A3 to B3): Guess who's skipped out on the show? Actually, we don't know her but she looked friendly enough. Nos. 2 and 3 (A4): Stripes beat poles, and orange sweatshirts morph into purple ones every time. Them's the rules. No. 4 (C1): Bald men of the world, cast off your hats! No. 5 (C2): He's got the biggest wheel in town, or at least under the tent. No. 6 (C2 to D2): Time to call out the rope repair crew. Nos. 7, 8, and 9 (C3): Better luck next time. Not only is he rolling backward, he's also lost his skull. Not in his head, silly, on his bike. Well, at least he's gained a watch. No. 10 (C5): This bike is a little hard to handle. Nos. 11 and 12 (D4): The big, black box is a little bigger now. Maybe that's why that clump of copper-colored disks—could they be coins? Whatever. Clump of sumpin'—on top has slipped around. No. 13 (D5): The reflection has lost its connection. No. 14 (E4): This fender feels quite protective of its wheel.

Page 98: Fixer-Uppers No. 1 (A1 to A2): The window is feeling the force of gravity. No. 2 (A4): It's a quadra-optic birdhouse. No. 3 (B1): Road signage theft is a problem in these parts. No. 4 (B2 to B3): The tree's shadow has been trunk-ated. No. 5 (B4): The pole vaulted in front of the bell. No. 6 (C1): You can really stretch out in this bathtub. No. 7 (C1 to D1): We dot no *i* before its time. No. 8 (C1 to E2): This sign just keeps on growing. No. 9 (C3 to C4): My, that's a long log you have. No. 10 (C4): It takes a missing leg to tip a table down. It's tippy now, but it'll soon be falling. No. 11 (D1): The arrow has been shafted. No. 12 (D2): It's a new concept in merchandising. They sell one item and then close up shop. No. 13 (D2 to D3): A can of spray paint, and what was red is now blue. No. 14 (D3): Buyer beware. This frame is a cross-piece fleece. No. 15 (D4): All together now: "Let the sun shine in!" We can't hear you. We still can't hear you. Oh, never mind.

Page 100: Iron Chef No. 1 (A1): The lamp shade's lattice frame has a slat that's slightly long. No. 2 (A2 to B2): A light's reflection has gradually lessened, and now it's completely gone. Nos. 3 and 4 (A3): The copper head-dress on the robo-waiter is lopsidedly tall, and if you thought it had a hole, you'd certainly be wrong. No. 5 (A4): Two more lights, that's nice.

No. 6 (B2 to C2): There's room at the table for one more. No. 7 (B3): If you keep crossing your eyes, they're going to stay that way. That's better. No. 8 (B5): She's out of here. No. 9 (C2): What was our waiter's name again? Nos. 10 and 11 (C3): He's so happy about earning another gold blobby thingie that he's dishing out more meat. Nos. 12, 13, and 14 (C4): Our tin man appears to like the soulful sounds of Detroit, has knocked down a metal post, and has borrowed all the meat from one of the bowls. Now we know where the extra serving came from! No. 15 (C5): The steel bar has been further incised. No. 16 (D3): The reflected claw appears to be anticipating movement in its brother claw above.

Page 102: A Favorable Wind
One of the men in photo No. 3 has ducked his head behind a kite. Look closely and you'll see it's true.

Page 103: On a Wing and a Prayer
In photo No. 6 the tailpipe—well, it's not really a tailpipe . . . fuselage pipe? Okay, the pipe with all the smoke coming out of it—is an incy wincy bit smaller. We'll bet finding it was exhausting (pun intended).

Page 104: In-Flight Dining No. 1 (A2): The building's outside design is being renewed. No. 2 (A5): Say goodbye to another window. Don't worry, it's the last time in this book. No. 3 (B1): The new skylight is the two-pane model. No. 4 (B5 to C5): We made no promises about flipping windows! No. 5 (C1): This guest bears a striking resemblance to another high diner. Nos. 6 and 7 (C1 to D1): The car drove up so fast, the streetlight spun around. Nos. 8 and 9 (C2): Could there be a safety reason why the off-brand seat is empty? Never mind, what they don't know won't hurt them. As for the rest, let them drink champagne. Nos. 10 and 11 (C3): Another diner has joined the crowd, just as the chef pulls out the big whisk. *Hmm.* Maybe he doesn't like late arrivals. No. 12 (C4 to D4): That pole was a redundant support. Excuse us, we've got to leave now. No. 13 (D2): The green dot is coming down with a bad case of wanderlust. No. 14 (D4): One of these chairs provides solid back support. No. 15 (D5): A chimney has toppled into the park. No. 16 (E2 to E3): Someone's been soldering in the hollows in the beam.

Page 106: Cheek to Jowl No. 1 (A2 to B2): An all-green shoe removes any risk of unintended product placement—and has quite a lovely Irish Spring appearance as well. (We hope our check is on the way.) No. 2 (A2): Hiked-up socks are so attractive—*not.* Nos. 3 and 4 (A3): The junction box is now well-screwed, but without a clip, the BX cable may swing. No. 5 (A4): Don't worry, he's got his thumb on the problem. No. 6 (B2 to B3): The greenish hue appears to be spreading from shoe to shoe. No. 7 (C3): After a stunt like this, it's a well-deserved star. No. 8 (C3 to D3): Polydactyly is somewhat impractical unless the offending digit can move around. If fully functional, it may have merit, as any 12-fingered pianist will attest. No. 9 (C4): It's not very polite to prefer a foot over a face. No. 10 (C4 to C5): Brickwork yet again. *Yawn.* No. 11 (D2): It may

be a bit more subtle, but it's still just two more blocks. Or rather, one. Okay, yes, a brick, a brick. Nos. 12 and 13 (D3): A knee just wants to be free, and that's what they call deep soul. No. 14 (E3): The mortar has been routed away. Nos. 15 and 16 (E3 to E4): With those extra stripes, what would you make that to be, a size 11 or 12?

Page 108: Right of Way No. 1 (A2 to B2): Without something to prop it up, the canopy above must soon recline. No. 2 (A5): Falling urns might be considered an architectural danger. No. 3 (A5 to B5): We lied about the windows. No. 4 (B3): The building is getting a face-lift. No. 5 (B5 to C5): New shades are also being installed. No. 6 (C1): If I were you, I wouldn't trust that rail. No. 7 (C1 to C2): You don't have to visit Moscow to see a red square. No. 8 (C3): This lamp can't be topped. No. 9 (C4): This tusk was made for jutting. No. 10 (C5): The sphere is balling up. No. 11 (D1): When the stone slab shifted, it must have cracked. No. 12 (D2): In a dramatic reversal of entropy, the wooden leg has grown together. Soon, ice cream colds will spontaneously get colder and messy boys' rooms will clean themselves. Dream on. Nos. 13 and 14 (D3): A defiant *E* faces the other way, as an awning takes advantage of the chaos to claim more territory. No. 15 (D4): The traffic lights are putting out contradictory signals. Nos. 16 and 17 (E1): While someone's suddenly gone bald, another man is the face *not* in the crowd. No. 18 (E3): Now, this *is* the face in the crowd. No. 19 (E3 to E4): The subway isn't public anymore. No. 20 (E4): It's either reverse entropy again or someone is about to make a fortune with a baldness cure.

[LIFE CLASSICS]

Page 111: Will Work for Peanuts No. 1 (A3): One flag down, nine more to go. No. 2 (A5): What's the point in racing toward a steeple? No. 3 (B1): This sign makes lots of weak promises. No. 4 (B2): Someone must think large posters get more attention. They probably do. No. 5 (B4): The dome gets the (new) point. No. 6 (C2 to D2): It does no good to shake a stick at an elephant. Canes don't work either. We've tried. No. 7 (E1 to E2): There are more stairs there. No. 8 (E2): Scandalous—she's showing off a little boot. No. 9 (E3): Luckily only the shadow lost her head. No. 10 (E5): It's just a shadow of a tail.

Page 112: Strategic Air Command No. 1 (A4): Little Jack Horner decided not to stick out his thumb after all. No. 2 (B3 to C3): He's quietly reaching for one of the planes. No. 3 (B3): The plane seems eager to be caught. No. 4 (B5): Don't worry. He hasn't lost a foot, he's just slipped it in under the table. Probably. No. 5 (C1 to D1): How do you pull open the drawer now? No. 6 (C1 to D2): His hair auditioned for a new part. Nos. 7 and 8 (C4): One plane is showing off its wider wings, while the other has scared off its own shadow. No. 9 (E3): We won't make any promises, but these are the last missing buttons in the book. We promise. No. 10 (E4): He taps his fingers when he's restless. No. 11 (E5): Someone's dad is going to be mad when he finds out about the broken tools.

Page 114: Aqua-Cat No. 1 (A2 to A3): Note: 1 plus 1 makes 11. It's the *new* new math. Nos. 2 and 3 (B1): As *X* takes a little spin, a feline brother takes a look through the porthole. No. 4 (B3): Before they embark on their mission, somebody needs to put the *N* back in NAVY. No. 5 (B4): And fix that *V* at the same time. No. 6 (B5): Need a tip? We've got one we stole from this photo. Also, buy high and sell low. No. 7 (C3): The stitching has worn away. No. 8 (C3 to C4): He's a cool, cool cat. No. 9 (E5): The slab is shorter than it was yesterday.

Page 116: Heaven's Angels Nos. 1, 2, and 3 (B2): Let's peel off three quick answers: Rogaine or rug? Only his hairdresser knows for sure. This fellow's hair is blowing in the wind. And he appears to have headlight envy—now fixed. Nos. 4 and 5 (B3): Of course she's the leader, she's the one with the big hair. But he had to look away. No. 6 (B4): I feel the sign move under my feet. Wait, that makes no sense. Still, the sign is moving. No. 7 (C1): Here's hoping she doesn't need to stop suddenly. Or ever. No. 8 (C2): She doesn't just have a handle on things, she's got it covered. The handle, we mean. No. 9 (C3): She doesn't just lead the gang, now she lights the way. No. 10 (D1): This lady must have been recently bitten. She's going vamp on us. Nos. 11 and 12 (D5): Not only does she need a fender vendor now, she's also going to have a hard time staying within the lines.

Page 118: Under the Big Top No. 1 (A1 to A2): Maybe the acrobats can fix that light while they're up there swinging around. No. 2 (B2 to C2): In case of trouble, he can just grab the rope. But what is she going to do? Nos. 3 and 4 (B3): The swing looks a bit dodgy, but never mind. It's her outfit that's getting all the attention. No. 5 (C1 to E2): Here's a chimp who is clearly on the move. No. 6 (C3): Let's give him a really big hand. Oh, we did. No. 7 (D1 to D2): The position of the curtain seems a little uncertain. No. 8 (D2): When are they going to get that horse back in harness? No. 9 (D4): These rings are definitely unparalleled.

A Devilish Cycle

This rider is going nowhere fast

MICHAEL URBAN/AFP/GETTY

11
changes

KEEP
SCORE

☐
☐
☐
☐
☐
☐
☐
☐
☐
☐
☐

⧖

3min 35sec

A
—
B
—
C
—
D
—
E

1 | 2 | 3 | 4 | 5

Solve this and become a true puppet, I mean, puzzle master.

ANSWERS No. 1 (A2): The end of the pipe has been capped. **No. 2 (B2):** There's been a tube switcheroo. **Nos. 3 and 4 (B3):** The flag has been restriped and stretched. **No. 5 (C3):** This *U* won't hold water. **No. 6 (C5):** If they keep growing, his devilish horns will need to be filed down. **No. 7 (D3):** An extra spoke won't help this contraption get going. **No. 8 (D4):** Oh, no. It's thumbs down. **No. 9 (D5):** The roses are blowing backward in the breeze. **No. 10 (E2):** The barn is windowless. **No. 11 (E5):** With all the pumping, his sneaker has earned its extra stripe.